IMAGES OF ENGLAND

AROUND
RICKMANSWORTH

IMAGES OF ENGLAND

AROUND RICKMANSWORTH

DENNIS F. EDWARDS

The
History
Press

First published in 1996 by Tempus Publishing Limited

Reprinted in 2011 by

The History Press
The Mill, Brimscombe Port,
Stroud, Gloucestershire, GL5 2QG
www.thehistorypress.co.uk

British Library Cataloguing in Publication Data.
A catalogue record for this book is available from the British Library.

ISBN 978 0 7524 0660 2

Typesetting and origination by Tempus Publishing Limited
Printed in Great Britain

Contents

Acknowledgements

I would like to acknowledge the following for permission to use their photographs:

Hertfordshire Records Office,
Three Rivers Museum Society,
W.J. Haynes,
J.F. Higham.

PUBLISHER'S NOTE

When the author retired at the end of 1998, he planned to devote more time to carrying out further local history research with a view to writing more books. Sadly, within months of his retirement he fell victim to multiple myeloma and was never able to fulfil his ambition. He passed away in 2004.

Introduction

Rickmansworth has been called 'the gateway to the Chilterns'; a frontier town set amid many waterways and bordered by the counties of Middlesex and Buckinghamshire. To travellers on the old Metropolitan and Great Central Joint Railway (later LNER), it was the place where one's train changed its motive power from electric to steam for the pull up through the deep chalk cutting to Chorleywood, and on to the heart of the Chilterns.

Rickmansworth is derived from 'Ryckmer', the name of some Saxon family head or chief and 'worth' which means farm (or, more probably, a stockade in which both early Saxon settlers and their animals lived). The Domesday Survey (1086) lists the settlement as the Manor of Prichemaresworde. The manor was valued at £20 and contained four Frenchmen (Normans) and forty-one labourers.

One of the first references to a church here was in 1219, when Pope Honorius III confirmed the church to the Abbey of St Albans. It seems that Rickmansworth was of sufficient importance to be granted a Market Charter in 1542. A market hall was built in the middle of High Street approximately opposite the modern post office. There was a structure here until 1806, when it was dismantled and moved to the south side of the street because of an all too familiar reason – the pressure of traffic! The Chess, the Gade and the Colne provided power for the many mills around the area and by the eighteenth century, paper was also being manufactured. Rickmansworth was comparable in size and importance to Watford, although the latter town had one advantage – it was on an important roadway to the Midlands – especially with the increase in stage coach traffic.

The construction of the Grand Junction Canal linking London and Birmingham in 1796 brought Rickmansworth prosperity but this was eclipsed by the opening, through Watford, of the London and Birmingham Railway (later the London and North Western Railway) in 1837/38 and Rickmansworth was left isolated. The town thus remained compact and retained its old fashioned houses and shops. Rickmansworth's first railway was the branch line from Watford to Church Street of 1862, sponsored by Lord Ebury of Moor Park who had an ambitious plan to extend the link down the Colne valley to Uxbridge where it would link with the GWR at Vine Street. It would have been a useful route and Ebury looked to a day when the quality coal of South Wales could be brought direct to Rickmansworth. The branch was never a success and it was not until 1889 that a direct rail connection to the heart of London was made when the Metropolitan Railway's extension line from Harrow and Baker Street arrived. The owners of Rickmansworth Park refused to sell their land, so the line had to curve sharply round into the Chilterns, with expensive cuttings through the chalk. Lord Ebury also refused to sell land at Moor Park and the line from London had to curve round the northern boundary of the estate.

When the Great Central trains began using the Metropolitan route to reach the new Marylebone station (London's last terminus) in 1899, Rickmansworth was on the main line railway map (although the fast expresses ran non-stop through the station). By the end of the century the first commuters were moving to Rickmansworth – and particularly to the wooded delights of Chorleywood. Rickmansworth and district also became a popular place for visitors who were increasingly encouraged to take a trip on the new railway by cheap ticket offers. Tea rooms and improved public houses were developed to cater for this trade. Local photographers began to record the local scene and the first picture postcard appeared just over a century ago. The locks at Batchworth were a favourite subject as were High Street and the breezy grasslands of Chorleywood and Croxley. However, at the outbreak of the First World War, the great country estates in the area were still in private hands: Moor Park; Rickmansworth Park; The Bury; Moneyhill; Glen Chess; Loudwater; Chorleywood House and the Cedars.

Despite its commercial traffic, the canal was an attraction for visitors in Edwardian days (as it still is now). The writer Herbert Tomkins' Highways and Byways in Hertfordshire recalled the pleasures of 'the monkey barges drawing up beside the towing path ... a few sand martins darting hither and thither erratically as bats; a canary and lark singing by turns in their cages over the doorway of the White Bear, their voices hardly audible at times above the roar of the water of the lock.'

The electrification of the Metropolitan Railway to Rickmansworth, and the building of its branch from Moor Park and from Rickmansworth to Watford (Cassiobury Park), began the development of modern Rickmansworth and Chorleywood. The Metropolitan Railway Country Estates Company was formed in 1919 to purchase and develop land near the line for housing. Its highly successful 'Live in Metroland' campaign brought many new residents. Even historic Moor Park was sold by the Grosvenor family and much of the land laid out with high class residences by Lord Leverhulme's Moor Park Estate Company. Yet all these developments did not affect the old town centre, which has only seen change in the past thirty-five years. In 1939 Rickmansworth still had a country town atmosphere and the old Hertfordshire dialect was heard in its streets.

Today, most of the landmarks and interesting features have been swept away – many to keep traffic moving. The ever-changing pattern of commerce in the 1990s has resulted in most of the old business names disappearing: Walkers boat and timber yards is now a Tesco and Franlin's site, a Marks and Spencer. This collection of pictures opens a window to those days before the great changes of the last century. Some of them date back only thirty years ago. How things have changed since then! The first modern shopping precinct, Penn Place, now has a very sorry aspect, as does The Bury, all boarded up and forlorn. But I have a feeling that, for many years yet, it will still be possible to amble along the canal tow path and watch the pleasure boats glide past. Or savour the fresh air of Chorleywood Common and the open vista of Croxley Green. Let us hope that at least these things will continue unchanged.

Dennis F. Edwards
February 1996, Uxbridge

One

Churches and Houses

A distant prospect of the town of Rickmansworth, published in December 1778. The sailing boat on the Colne is artistic licence but as early as 1641 there were plans for improving the river for navigation down to Uxbridge and London.

The foundation of St Mary's goes back at least to the thirteenth century. The church was rebuilt twice in 1630 and in Victorian days. The architect for the present building was Sir Arthur Blomfield.

St Mary's church from Church Street. The Feathers public house and the adjacent property date from the seventeenth century. The church tower (restored in 1930) is one of the only remains of the ancient building.

ckmansworth, St. Mary's Church Chancel.

The east window seen here is by Edwin Burne-Jones from 1891 and commemorates the first Earl of Monmouth. He had the challenging task of riding from Richmond Palace to Scotland to tell King James that Queen Elizabeth had died.

The Bury was the ancient Manor House of Rickmansworth. The building seen here dates from 1627, when it was constructed by Sir Gilbert Wakering on the site of an older building. In 1682 the Bury passed to the Fotherley family.

The Bury in more modern times was the home of the eccentric but respected Thomas William Bevan, organist of Watford Parish Church. The house was an administrative centre for the Civil Defence in the Second World War and later a Hertfordshire County Council health centre. It is now empty and in a poor state of repair.

A pleasant view of the Bury around 1914. A 300-yard long canal branch (or 'arm') was dug through part of the grounds in 1845 to serve the bakery of John Taylor. Much of the secluded atmosphere was lost when the Riverside Way by-pass was cut through twenty years ago.

Basing House is one of the best-known buildings in the town. The house was constructed in 1740 on the site of the house where William Penn and his wife, Gulielma lived from 1672–76. Additions were made in the early nineteenth century and the house became a school by 1839. A century ago it was owned by Roderick William Henderson, a local JP. It became council offices in 1930 and part now houses the excellent Three Rivers Museum.

Rickmansworth Park dominated the town for several centuries. The mansion in this picture was built in 1740 and by 1813 was the home of the High Sheriff, Henry Whitfield, and later, the Birch family. Deer were once a familiar sight but they appear to have been replaced by sheep in this 1906 photograph.

A tranquil scene in Rickmansworth Park, 1905 – from a postcard published by Thomas Price of Station Road.

The park was sold in 1926 by Viscountess Barrington (formerly Mrs Joan Birch). The old house was demolished and replaced by the Royal Masonic Institute for Girls.

Dining Hall of the Royal Masonic Institute for Girls' senior school around 1931.

The public were permitted to walk through the Park and here an Edwardian family are admiring the view. In the far distance in the great house itself.

The Loudwater entrance to Rickmansworth Park in 1902. The adjacent estate of Loudwater belonged at this time to James Haywood, one of the promoters of Christ Church, Chorleywood.

A morning gallop for troops of King Edward's Horse Artillery, who formed part of the Overseas Dominion Regiment. In 1914 the men were camped in various locations around Watford. Viscountess Barrington allowed them to use Rickmansworth Park. After one all-night exercise, she provided a nourishing breakfast for 300 officers and men.

Sergeant Major Byart in Rickmansworth Park, *c.* 1914.

The Roman Catholic church of Our Lady Help of All Christians seen from under the Metropolitan Railway bridge. The church dates from 1901.

The Roman Catholic church was built on the site of what had been Salters Malthouse and some of the buildings remained until 1995. The east window was dedicated in 1911 to Anne Sculley, wife of James Sculley, director of Salters Brewery.

Parsonage Farm was once part of the manor and was home of the Fotherley family from 1628. John White, a churchwarden at St Mary's parish church for fifty years, lived here in more recent times. The lands were developed by the Metropolitan Railway Country Estates in the period between the wars.

Two

Around the Town

View of the town from St Mary's tower – from a postcard sent by a French visitor to a friend in Paris in 1913. The trees surround the Old Rectory. The top of the picture shows the Metropolitan Railway goods warehouse; Solomon's Hill and the artists' rest home. In the distance are the unspoiled grounds of Rickmansworth Park.

Church Street and the junction with Talbot Road. The flags are for the Coronation of 1901. The Three Horseshoes public house is on the left.

Down to ground level and Church Street with the Priory and the Feathers public house. The street is recorded as early as 1332 as Churchestrat.

Beeson and Sons were purveyors of china, glass and other household items for many years on this corner. Talbot Road, at the side of the shop, was at one time called Redpale Road. On the right is the bridge over the ancient town ditch.

The same spot a few years later. The shop on the right, a rival to Beesons (left) is Davis Brothers, who sold ironmongery. Further down the street on the left is The Chequers Inn, now a restaurant.

Forty years later – Beesons are still on the corner, with Davis' opposite. Barrett, the baker and The Chequers Inn on the left. In the distance, on the right, is the Queens Arms and Bury Lane.

The famous Watersplash in Bury Lane where the town ditch crossed the roadway. Until 1799, the lane was the private drive from High Street to the Bury.

Braving the waters of Bury Lane! Newspaper delivery from Church Street station around 1910.

Parking was already becoming a problem when this photograph was taken of the Splash in the 1940s. The Beresford Almshouses are on the right. The original block, in High Street was erected for 'four poor persons' under the will of John Beresford (c. 1540–1663). The buildings seen here date from 1898.

RKS.49   WATER SPLASH, RICKMANSWORTH

The same spot in 1961, not long before the Splash was culverted over. Walking along this road in 1912, the writer Herbert Tomkins recalled, 'the bright clumps of myosotis and yellow marguerites in well-maintained beds in the front gardens of the almshouses.'

The corner of Church Street and High Street in 1901. The building on the right contained the post office. The buildings on the left were later demolished for modern shops.

High Street looking towards Church Street. The shop nearest the camera (on the right) was E.S. Brown 'stationer, fancy repository and circulating library. They were publishers of many postcard views of old Rickmansworth. Next door was Mungo Paterson, draper and tailor.

The Bell Inn around 1904. It was closed in 1912 and became the offices of Swannel and Sly, auctioneers and estate agents. The buildings were demolished in 1966–7 for the construction of Northway and new shops.

The Odeon Cinema and shops, opened in 1936. It was the more luxurious of the two Rickmansworth cinemas, the other being the Picture House at the far end of High Street by the railway bridge. The Picture House was owned by the Walter family and opened on 12 March 1927, closing in 22 June 1963. The Odeon lasted until 1964.

High Street with the entrance to the Town Hall on the left. The George public house on the right, and just beyond, Taylors boot and shoe shop, with its distinctive clock and boot sign, a landmark in High Street for many years.

The Swan Hotel was, perhaps, the most well known of the Rickmansworth inns. It was a posting house on the road to Aylesbury and Bicester, and is first mentioned by name in 1665. As recently as 1952 it advertised itself as 'a comfortable hotel of distinction.' With adjacent property, it was demolished in 1964 making way for modern shops, including the post office.

The yard of the Swan Inn, once a bustling place when coaches such as The Accommodation called in on its daily journey from Amersham to London in pre-railway days.

High Street, Rickmansworth.

A fine view of life in High Street in the years just before the First World War. On the left is Rickmansworth's first cinema. The Electric Picture Palace, into which the old Town Hall was converted. Opening in 1912, the cinema last until 1927 when the Picture House opened at the Croxley end of High Street. The Swan Hotel and the post office are on the right.

High Street, Rickmansworth.

The same spot in 1955. T. Walton, a high class fruiters which once had shops all over London and surrounding counties, has replaced the frontage of the old Town Hall and cinema (left). On the other side of the street, the clock and boot are still in place above the shoe shop.

High Street in the 1920s with Brown and Sons the printers and stationers and the old post office. Despite the early suburban developments at that time, Rickmansworth still had a country town atmosphere and many of the people seen here would have retained their Hertfordshire accents.

The town was an increasingly popular place for day visitors – especially those who came by the new electric trains. Beasley's was a popular local venue for refreshments in the 1920s.

RKS 53   High Street, Rickmansworth.

A view from the 1960s, W.H. Smiths was built on the site of old cottages next to the Fotherley Almshouses. On the very edge of this picture to the right can be seen W.H. Cullen, the grocer, a company that at one time had many branches in local towns.

The Fotherley Almshouses around 1900. They were built in 1682 for 'five poor widows'. Woolworths opened on the site on 9 March 1934 but closed in 1971.

High Street at the junction of Bury Lane, with the old Cart and Horses, now demolished. A number of once well known shopping names can be seen: MacFisheries, Eastmans butchers and Achille Sierre, dry cleaners. Posters are advertising Soldiers Three at the Odeon and a musical at the Palace Theatre in Watford.

The London and County Bank, (now Natwest Bank) decorated for the coronation for Edward VII. At the time of this picture, the banking hours were daily 10 am to 4 pm and Saturdays, 10 am to 1 pm.

A last glimpse of the coronation celebrations nearly a century ago. Thomas Goodyear, the butcher, is on the left. At the far end is what was, until 1898, High Street West (hence the Western Inn).

Station Road was originally called Keeper Hill because it led to the cottage where the Bailiff of Rickmansworth Park lived. The coming of the Metropolitan Railway changed all that in the late 1880s. George Sumner's pharmacy, one of the shops on the left, was still in business until 1989.

Station Road in the 1960s before the great changes took place. The Metropolitan Railway bridge has been rebuilt, but you can just see 'The Homestead' beyond, now the giant office block which houses Comet Warehouses and other international companies. Most of these buildings were demolished in 1962–3 for the Penn Place Shopping Centre. It was named by the developer after William Penn: 'a man of energetic and sound commercial integrity-applicable to a development such as we seek create'. Nearly twenty five years later, the precinct lies more or less derelict.

There was time to stand in the road when this scene of Station Road was photographed by Mr Price, whose shop can be seen on the left, in Edwardian days. The original Metropolitan Railway bridge and the boundary of Rickmansworth park can be seen in the distance.

RKS.44 STATION ROAD FROM BRIDGE, RICKMANSWORTH

Under the bridge and round to the by-pass, *c*. 1958. The original by-pass was built in the 1930s and earth was placed in Rickmansworth Park and landscaped. The new road cut off the old park from the town. Further widening and the huge new roundabout were built in the 1960s and more improvements made in the 1970s.

It is difficult today to imagine Rickmansworth as a holiday resort. But the coming of the Metropolitan and later, the trains of the Great Central Railway, offered tired Londoners a chance to spend a day or weekend in the country. Hotels such as the Victoria were opened at this time.

44

Chorleywood Road was originally Chorleywood Lane and the council proposed re-naming it Victoria Road (after the hotel) in 1898. The Cemetery, on the left, opened in 1856. The flint cottage was the home of George Kempster, the Superintendent.

Right: Information for intending residents, published by the Metropolitan Railway Country Estates Company in 1924.

LOCAL DATA, Etc.

RICKMANSWORTH

TRAINS, EACH WAY, DAILY	46
JOURNEY TIME TO BAKER STREET ...	27 mins.
LOCAL RATES IN THE £	9 10
GAS, PER THERM	1 0½
CHARGES FOR WATER	5% on gross value
ELECTRIC LIGHT, PER UNIT	*8d.
ALTITUDE	250 feet

CHORLEY WOOD

TRAINS, EACH WAY, DAILY	39
JOURNEY TIME TO BAKER STREET ...	34 mins.
LOCAL RATES IN THE £	9 10
GAS PER THERM	1 2½
CHARGES FOR WATER	5% on gross value
ELECTRIC LIGHT PER UNIT	*8d.
ALTITUDE	350 feet

* Or a flat rate of 1d. per unit subject to fixed charge.

Examples of SEASON TICKET RATES operating between Rickmansworth and the undermentioned stations.

TO	Third Class		First Class	
	3 months	1 month	3 months	1 month
	£ s. d.	£ s. d.	£ s. d.	£ s. d.
WILLESDEN GREEN ...	3 13 0	1 9 6	6 5 3	2 6 0
BAKER STREET ...	4 13 6	1 16 3	7 7 9	2 14 3
KING'S CROSS ...	5 3 9	1 18 6	7 16 9	2 17 6
FARRINGDON & H.H. ...	5 7 6	1 19 6	8 1 3	2 19 3
LIVERPOOL STREET ...	5 10 6	2 0 9	8 5 9	3 1 0
ALDGATE ...	5 10 6	2 0 9	8 5 9	3 1 0
PADDINGTON (PRAED STREET) (BISHOPS ROAD) ...	5 1 6	1 17 3	7 12 3	2 16 0
KENSINGTON (HIGH STREET) ...	5 7 6	1 19 6	8 1 3	2 19 3
OXFORD CIRCUS ...	5 5 0	2 0 3	7 19 3	2 18 3
PICCADILLY CIRCUS ...	5 16 0	2 4 3	8 10 3	3 2 3

Opposite: Early view of the Victoria Hotel. The adjacent Park View Hotel was originally Park View House and closed around thirty five years ago. Unlike the Victoria, it was not licensed. The Victoria had a spacious ball room which could accommodate 300 dancers and a spacious lock-up garage for motors. Both establishments were owned by the Sedgewick family.

A Garden Fete
—and Sale—

WILL BE HELD ON

WEDNESDAY, 14th JUNE, 1911,

From 3 p.m. to 7.30 p.m. at

Moneyhill House, Rickmansworth,

(By kind permission of Mrs. Alfred Loder).

To reduce the debt on the Catholic Church, Rickmansworth.

THE COUNTESS OF DENBIGH

has kindly consented to open the proceedings.

A BAND WILL PLAY DURING THE AFTERNOON.

FANCY STALL.—Mrs. and Miss Bridgland.
LUCKY DIP.—Mrs. Gerald Hoare.
PARCELS & PACKING.—Mrs. and Miss Kernan.
WHITE STALL,—Mrs. Alfred Loder.
CHINA & GLASS.—Lady Ellen Lambart.
STATIONERY, ETC.—Mrs. Leeming.
SCENT, SOAP, & BASKETS.—Mrs. O'Connell and Mrs. Collins.
FRUIT, FLOWERS, & DAIRY PRODUCE.—Mrs. Philip Thornton.
BOOKS & SACRED PICTURES.—The Convent School.

DRAMATIC AND OTHER ENTERTAINMENTS.
LUCKY WHEEL, COCOANUT SHIES, ETC,

Routes from London for Motors, 17 miles via Edgware, Stanmore and Bushey, 20 miles via Uxbridge. Train leaves Marylebone G.C. Station at 2 o'clock; Baker St., Met. (changing at Harrow) at 1.45. Moneyhill House is about 15 minutes walk from Met. and G.C. and the L.N.W. Station from Watford.

Entrance 2s. Children Half-price. After 6 p.m. 6d.

Tickets can be obtained at Gate, or previously from the Hon. Sec..—Mrs. Loder, Moneyhill House, or the Hon. Treas. :—Mrs. Thornton, Parsonage Farm, Rickmansworth.

Brown & Son, Rickmansworth.

A fund raising garden fête at Money Hill House. In the 1900s it was the home of Thomas Andrews, a director of Harland and Wolff, the ship builders. He was one of the designers of the 'unsinkable' Titanic and perished with her in 1912. After the First World War, the house became a hotel for a short time, the estate then being purchased by the Metropolitan Railway Country Estates for development.

Housing development in the area began in the early 1920s. This is the cover for the Cedar Estate brochure of 1927, published by the Metropolitan Railway Country Estates.

CEDARS ESTATE
RICKMANSWORTH
HERTFORDSHIRE

YOUR IDEAL HOME awaits you at
RICKMANSWORTH (on the Cedars Estate)
and the intending Purchaser could do no better than select one of the splendid HOUSES built by

J. W. MINETT,
and rely upon QUALITY—DISTINCTION—HONEST VALUE —SUPERIOR WORKMANSHIP & ARTISTIC APPEARANCE

Semi-Detached from £790 to £1050 Freehold
Detached from £950 to £1375 Freehold
Plots approximately 30ft., by 150ft. and 33ft. to 36ft., by 160ft. respectively. Space for Garage.
NO ROAD OR LEGAL CHARGES.
Accommodation : 2 Reception, 3 and 4 Bedrooms; Bathroom, Kitchen, Cloak Room, and 2 Lavatories. Also Garage or space for same.
All the rooms are commodious, and every modern Labour Saving convenience are fitted to every House.
A VISIT WILL CONVINCE YOU.
ESTATE OFFICE is 3rd Turning on Right past War Memorial
or further particulars of these charming houses gladly supplied on application to :
Mr. J. W. MINETT,
"HOMELANDS,"
PARKWAY, RICKMANSWORTH, HERTS.
Tel. : Rickmansworth 608.

Ideal homes in semi-rural Metroland shown in a advertisement from 1930.

Houses in Highfield Way, a development of the Metropolitan Railway Country Estates, 1930. 'They are all brick-built and erected under the supervision of the Company's architect, and no effort is spared in giving purchasers the maximum of satisfaction and value'. The architect was the railway's C.W. Clark, who also designed Croxley Green and Watford Metropolitan stations.

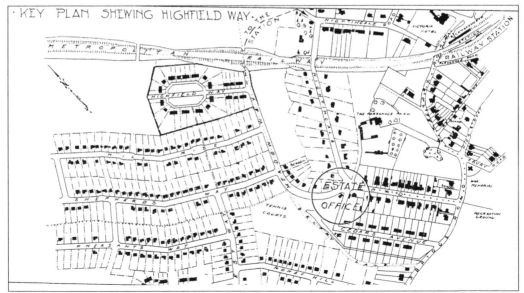

Plan of the Metropolitan estate at Highfield Way. The Moneyhill shopping parades on the Uxbridge Road were begun in 1928.

48

Live at Rickmansworth – the mid 1930s were the golden age of Metroland. Houses of all kinds and at all prices were built by the hundreds along the Metropolitan Railway. Advertisement from one of the London evening newspapers.

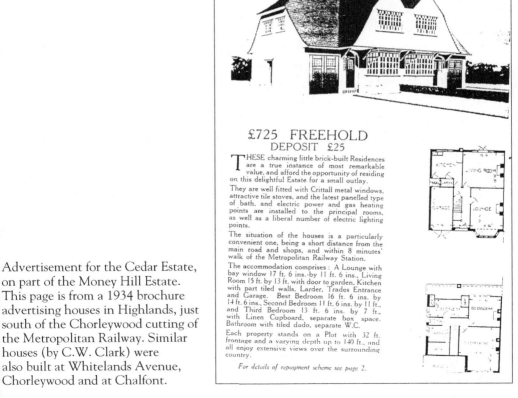

Advertisement for the Cedar Estate, on part of the Money Hill Estate. This page is from a 1934 brochure advertising houses in Highlands, just south of the Chorleywood cutting of the Metropolitan Railway. Similar houses (by C.W. Clark) were also built at Whitelands Avenue, Chorleywood and at Chalfont.

£1250 FREEHOLD. DEPOSIT £50

IN this property the same principles of planning and design have been followed, providing a particularly pleasing effect, and an Oriel window has been introduced to the front. The solid character of the roof will be recognised as a successful feature, in which hand-made sand-faced tiles and bonnet hips have been used. The internal fittings, stoves, etc., have also been well chosen, and due regard paid to all labour-saving devices.

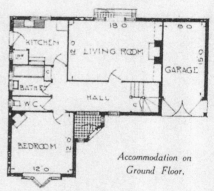

Accommodation on Ground Floor.

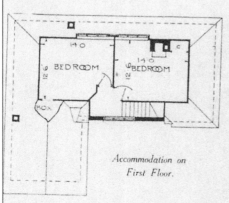

Accommodation on First Floor.

The accommodation comprises :—

A well-proportioned Living Room, 18 ft. by 12 ft., Hall, Bedroom, 12 ft. by 12 ft., with Oriel window; Bathroom, with tiled dado and panelled bath, fitted lavatory basin, separate W.C.; Kitchen, with tiled dado and Larder. Two good bedrooms above, each 14 ft. by 12 ft. 6 ins., and a large Box space. Garage at side, 15 ft. by 8 ft. Includes a well-wooded site with 50 ft. frontage to Moor Lane. No Road charges. Main drainage. Electric power and lighting points.

Moor Lane Estate on the other side of the town at Batchworth was another Metropolitan estate development. The price of £1250 was fairly expensive in 1934.

Three

Canal and Rivers

One of the earliest views of Batchworth Locks and the Mills, *c*. 1819. The Grand Junction Canal opened through Rickmansworth in September 1797. In his book A Tour of the Grand Junction Canal, published in 1819, John Hassell recorded 'a little inn at Batchworth kept by a butcher as well as a vintner, and where twice in my life I have dined off the best mutton chops I ever tasted.'

Rickmansworth. Batchworth.

Batchworth Mills were owned by Thomas Buller in 1759 and produced silk and cloth. The mills were purchased by John Dickinson, the paper maker, in 1818. The mills closed in 1910 and were largely demolished for the building of the Rickmansworth and Uxbridge Valley waterworks. The house on the right was the Dower House of the Eburys of Moor Park. All the buildings here have been demolished for road widening.

Batchworth locks have been photographed many times. Here canal craft are passing through during the First World War.

A slightly later view of Batchworth Locks. The lock has a capacity of 60,000 gallons and the rise of the waterway is 6ft 8in.

Batchworth Locks in the early 1920s. The left hand waterway leads to the Salters Arm, a short length of the River Chess that was canalised to serve the brewery and the gas works. The Rickmansworth Gas Company opened in 1852 and sometimes this waterway is called the Gas Works Arm.

Gravel extraction has long been a local industry. This is the pit of the Rickmansworth Sand and Gravel Company, with wagons of the Metropolitan Railway. The gravel company advertised in 1905 (around the time this view was taken), that it could execute 'prompt delivery to all stations on the Metropolitan Railway'. It is not known exactly where the rail connection joined the main railway.

The Railway Tavern and the bridge over the River Chess. The public house took its name from the Church Street terminus of the railway to Watford.

Frogmore Wharf and Walker's Yard. The company began building boats for the canal companies in 1907, when Frogmore was launched. It also built some of the first mechanically propelled boats. The last crafts built here were Aberystwyth and Bangor in 1952. The company then continued as timber merchants until closure in June 1989.

No. 8   Batchworth Lake, Rickmansw

Batchworth 'Lake' or the Aquadrome. Pleasure boats were rented here from late Edwardian days. The Walker family developed the gravel pit as a pleasure lake and operated the steam launch Gadfly on its waters. In the distance are the buildings of Frogmore Wharf.

Peaceful days beside the Colne in the 1930s. 'The Colne especially is a charming river; its waters are unpolluted. ...there are trout ...and an abundance of roach, perch and chub', professed a guide book in the 1920s.

Opposite: Frogmore Wharf and the yard of Walker Brothers. The company continued at this site as timber merchants until closure in June 1989. The yard is now occupied by a large Tesco store.

A somewhat romanticised view of the Colne near Rickmansworth around 90 years ago.

The year is 1924 and this peaceful scene on the Colne at Rickmansworth was used as publicity to attract Londoners to come out for the day by the train.

Boat traffic on the canal, c. 1922. Visitors to Rickmansworth in this period were recommended to walk along the tow path, 'and see the gaudily painted canal barges, each with its patient, plodding horse tugging at the tow rope, which can be seen passing to and for all day long'. Just visible are the chimney of the Sedgwick Brewery and the gables of The Elms. The tree in the foreground hides the less picturesque building of the gas works.

Commercial craft on the canal near Rickmansworth in 1924. A powered boat is towing a butty boat. All commercial traffic has now ceased on the canal, but it is a popular waterway for pleasure boats.

Rickmansworth, View on the Colne,

The Elms dates from 1720, and was the home of George Eliot (Mary Ann Evans) (1819–80). The house became a convent in 1922 and later the Joan of Arc School.

A London General Country Bus crosses Cassio Bridge on the border of Croxley and Watford, c. 1920. The bridge was partly rebuilt by the Hertfordshire County Council in 1922.

A panoramic view of Rickmansworth from the chimney of the old Batchworth Mills. This remarkable photograph was taken by T.J. Price in 1910, just before the old mills were demolished. On the far left is the old White Bear public house, dating from 1500, which was soon to be rebuilt. The bridge over the Colne dates from 1830. Batchworth lake can be seen and, in the distance, Moneyhill House at Mill End.

The long low building by the canal is part of The Boat Inn which had stables for the refreshment of canal horses. The LNWR Church Street station, the open water meadows and the Bury are visible to the left.

The third part of the panorama shows the main channel of the canal in the foreground and also the Rivers Colne and Chess, the latter serving as an 'arm' to the gas works (top right).

Four

Rail and Roads

Rickmansworth's first railway station was in Church Street – the terminus of which as affectionately called 'Lord Ebury's railway'. The line opened on 1 October 1862. It was intended to extend the railway down the valley to Uxbridge and link up with the Vine Street branch of the GWR. Lord Ebury promised a prosperous future if his plan was completed, 'the GWR will bring smokeless Welsh coal to the Chess and Colne valleys'. The station was rebuilt in 1927 when an electric train service commenced.

Oerlikon LMS electric trains such as this began running to Rickmansworth Church Street from 26 September 1927. There were never many passengers, the branch surviving because of its freight traffic. Closure was inevitable and passenger trains ran for the last time on 3 March 1952. 'A sad end to a valiant enterprise… a link with old Rickmansworth and days of gracious living when Lord and Lady Ebury lived at the Moor Park' said the local newspaper.

Mr A. Ingre and his railway delivery cart around 1905. In later years the yards were never busy, and became overgrown with grass. They finally closed on 2 January 1967.

The earliest known photograph of Rickmansworth Metropolitan station including a Beyer-Peacock type condensing locomotive and a train of 8-wheelers in 1887.

The old terminus at Church Street in the early 1950s, with a three-car 'Oerlikon' type electric train arriving from Watford.

Cattle pens and yards at the Metropolitan station with the town beyond, *c.* 1904.

A special train in the overgrown yards at Church Street terminus on 28 June 1958. The locomotive is a Stanier 0-4-4, No. 41901.

A rare picture of the station staff early this century. The small building, the water column, and the shrubs behind them were later removed for the bay line used by the Watford shuttle train.

G. C. Railway.—Manchester Express passing Rickmansworth.

When the Great Central Railway was extended down to London at the end of the century, its fast Manchester and Sheffield trains had to share track with the Metropolitan from Quainton Road to Harrow. Here a Manchester bound express passes the Rickmansworth goods shed.

THE METROPOLITAN RAILWAY COMPANY
BEGS TO ANNOUNCE THAT THE POPULAR
EXCURSIONS TO SEA SIDE
RESORTS ON THE SOUTH COAST
BY THROUGH TRAIN
From AYLESBURY, CHESHAM, RICKMANSWORTH, UXBRIDGE, &c.,
WILL COMMENCE EARLY IN JULY, 1913.
Full particulars will be announced later.

A day by the sea: advertisement, 1912-13.

With the advent of the First World War many troops were stationed in the area. Here members of the Artillery, Overseas Dominion Regiment are in the goods yard, now the station car park. At that time the trees of Rickmansworth Park bordered the yard.

Advertisement for Colin Taylor, corn and coal merchant. Another familiar sight at Metropolitan Railway yards was Alfred J. Pratt, supplier of building materials, with a depot at Rickmansworth.

The electrification of the Metropolitan Railway did much to encourage new settlers to come to Rickmansworth. Here Metro-Vickers electric locomotive Number 20 (later named *Dick Whittington*) waits for the return journey to Baker Street, conveying a special press party and high ranking officials of the Metropolitan and LNE railways. The electric trains began running to Rickmansworth on 5 January 1925.

The deserted down platform in 1934 – but the posters are full of interest. 'Linos, Carpets and Furniture' from B.B. Evans, a popular department store in Kilburn High Road. At this time many of the new house owners would have come from north-west London. But for local needs, there is an advertisement for Brandon and Sons, Chesham Broadway. Under the sign for Beefex are posters for the new sport of Speedway and a poster that reads, 'Give your dog a holiday too', at Heronsgate Kennels. The National Building Society (it was later to become the Abbey National) also advertise.

As the demand for houses increased in the 1930s, so did the amount of advertising. This is a press advertisement from 1933.

When the Metropolitan steam trains from Verney Junction and Aylesbury reached Rickmansworth, their locomotives were changed for electric traction. Here a Metropolitan 'H' class locomotive (built in 1922) arrives with a train from Aylesbury in 1935.

Uncoupling the steam locomotive and coupling on an electric locomotive could be achieved in about $4\frac{1}{4}$ minutes, it was claimed. Many a schoolboy would watch the operation with great interest from the platform.

Electric locomotive Number 3 *Sir Ralph Verney* is ready to leave. The Watford branch shuttle train can be seen on the far left. This service was withdrawn in 1934 because of bus competition.

A locomotive just uncoupled from a Baker Street train in April 1933. The house is the long vanished 'Homestead', which was the home of the Bailiff of Rickmansworth Park.

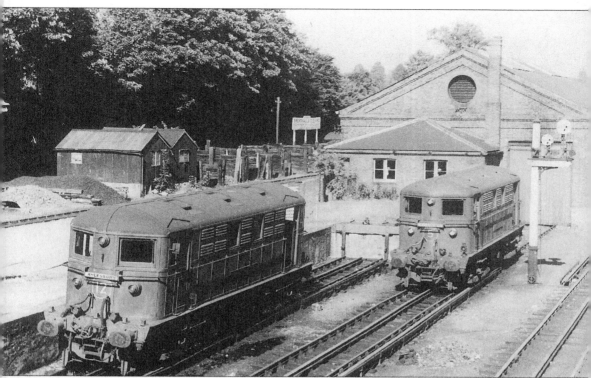

A familiar sight to all travellers for many years were the electric locomotives awaiting their turn outside the old goods shed, just south of the station. This picture was taken in 1951, with *Sarah Siddons* on the left and *John Hampden*. By chance, these are the only two remaining examples.

A rare photograph of Number 15 Wembley 1924 at Rickmansworth in the 1930s. The locomotive was actually exhibited at the 1925 British Empire Exhibition, with one side cut away to show visitors the electrical equipment. She was withdrawn from service on 18 September 1951.

Another unusual photograph of the regular operation at the Metropolitan station, 1950.
A special Sunday morning working of one of the Chesham branch sets, with an ex-Great
Central Railway (LNER) locomotive about to propel the train up the line to Chalfont and
Latimer.

Baker Street bound 'T' stock compartment electric train, with Number 14 *Benjamin Disraeli* just arrived with an Aylesbury train, c. 1955.

Opposite: The Marylebone suburban train approaching Rickmansworth in the 1950s. The goods yards at Rickmansworth were still in use at this time and the long-vanished yard water tower can just be seen at the top right.

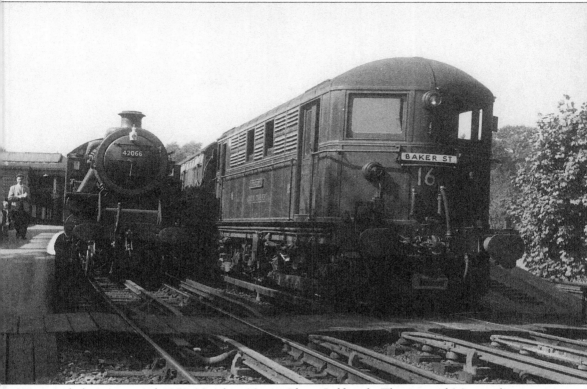

Steam and electric around 1959. Number 16 was *Oliver Goldsmith*. The original Metropolitan steam locomotives had all been withdrawn by this date.

Signs of change at the end of the 1950s – colour light signals. Number 5, *John Lyon* arrives from Baker Street by the old signal box.

Up the line now to Chorleywood. A goods train is steaming through on 2 June 1934 with a Metropolitan 'K' class locomotive of 1925.

Opposite: Metropolitan electric locomotives nos 18 (nearest camera) *Michael Faraday*, and 7, *Edmund Burke*. Both locomotives were scrapped at Rugby in July 1966. Note the goods siding on the right and the wooded heights of Moor Park in the distance.

CHORLEY WOOD HOTEL

CHORLEY WOOD.

Facing Station and adjoining Golf Course.

Fully Licensed Free Hotel.

Speciality—HOT LUNCHEONS DAILY.

Dinners, luncheons and teas served for small parties.

Situated on the Heights and the Centre for Rambles.

A. & A. E. GRIMMER.

The Chorleywood Hotel (now The Sportsman) – advertisement from 1924. The hotel had fourteen bedrooms and three sitting rooms and the latest amenities such as a billiards room and electric light.

Chorleywood station looking south in 1933. On the left platform can just be seen one of the new London Passenger transport signs. Note the milk churns, once a familiar sight on most country stations.

The wooden station at Moor Park first opened as Sandy Lodge, in 1910, but was enlarged in 1923 to serve the new housing developments. These were the 'wooden platforms crunched by hobnailed shoes... and this is where the healthier got out', according to Sir John Betjeman. The view here shows the old station a few years before it was rebuilt as a two-island station in conjunction with the quadrupling of the line in the early 1960s.

Great Central train between Northwood and Moor Park, *c.* 1910.

Building the Metropolitan Railway to Watford in 1923. This is the early work on the cutting through Croxley Hall Wood.

There were many heavy engineering works on the Watford branch line. Such as this bridge carrying Harvey Road over the future line. More than half a million cubic yards of soil and chalk had to be removed – the material going up the line to form the high embankments near the Watford terminus.

Croxley Green Station (now Croxley) with a special train carrying press and the officials of both the Metropolitan and LNER at the official opening ceremony. The line opened to the public on 2 November 1925. This train includes the Metropolitan's special carriage known as 'The Rothschild Saloon'.

Opposite: A bus operated by the Lewis Omnibus Company of Watford on the St Albans–Watford–Rickmansworth service, 3 July 1930.

MISSENDEN AND RICKMANSWORTH COACH

A picture of a stage coach in Edwardian days, when there was a brief revival by, what we would call today transport enthuisists, for the horse-drawn coaches. This is the old Berkeley Coach en route from Great Missenden to Rickmansworth in 1901. Apparently the jingle of its harness and the frequent noise made by its 'guard' blowing a traditional trumpet disturbed golfers and cricketers on Chorleywood Common.

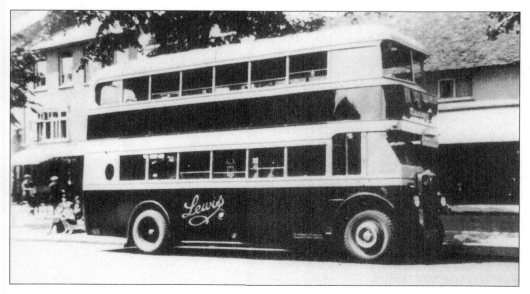

Mini-bus travel is not really a modern thing! Here is the Harefield to Rickmansworth bus about to leave Harefield village in 1933. It was one of a number of bus services operated by Filkins and Ainsworth. The routes to Uxbridge and Rickmansworth, which ran at three hourly intervals, were taken over by London Transport in 1933.

Another early bus route was the Loudwater bus which, by 1951, had become London Transport country bus route 336A. The service was begun in 1928 by Cameron Jeffs for the residents of his luxury Loudwater estate.

Bus services between Rickmansworth and Watford were operated by the National Bus Company and the Lewis Bus Company. They offered a cheaper and more direct way of getting to the centre of Watford than the shuttle train from Rickmansworth to the Metropolitan terminus on the edge of Cassiobury Park. This picture dates from the period just after the Second World War and shows a route 336 London Transport country bus outside Croxley Metropolitan station.

A 'Q' type bus at Rickmansworth by-pass, c. 1948. The route replaced the old Filkins and Ainsworth route, and ran up Woodcock Hill and Northwood Road to Harefield, then down Moorhall Road to Denham and Uxbridge.

A 'Farewell to Steam' special train on 9 September 1961, with the electric locomotive *Michael Faraday*. Seldom can the platforms at Rickmansworth have been so crowded, to say farewell to a piece of railway history. The author was travelling on this train.

Another view taken on the same day. Note the poster behind the ladies on the right, it advertises outings from London to King's Lynn for eighteen shillings, and Oxford for nineteen shillings.

Five

Chorleywood

Chorleywood Church and Rectory   Coles, Photographer, Watford

The northern edge of Chorleywood Common showing the old rectory. Chorleywood became a separate parish from Rickmansworth in 1845. Note the model horse and carts with which the boys are playing.

The first church was erected in 1845 and a contemporary writer described it as 'a neat, but unimposing structure'. Rebuilding took place in 1875, the architect being G.E. Street who was responsible for the law courts in London. The old tower was retained. The east window, dating from 1872, is in memory of John S. Gilliat and his wife, Louisa.

A quiet corner of Chorleywood in 1921 with some early suburban houses in what was then a still rural road.

A view of 1960–1 showing the Church School and Christ church. The school began in 1853, with 186 pupils. It was financed by the National Society for Promoting the Education of the Poor in the Principles of the Established Church. The buildings were enlarged in 1891 to allow for 200 pupils.

The Tollgate Inn as it was nearly a century ago. It took its name from the nearby tollgate established here under an Act of Parliament, 17 March 1768.

Tollgate Cottage on the corner of Dog Kennel Lane and Rickmansworth Road. Built in 1887, it was the home of Sir George and Lady Alexander. He was a theatrical producer and was associated with the productions of Sir Henry Irving at the Lyceum and the St James Theatre. He also produced many of Oscar Wilde's famous plays.

Another view of Tollgate Cottage from Dog Kennel Lane and the edge of the Common. Just to the left of the Tollgate Cottage is the top of Solesbridge Lane.

The pond beside Common Road near the junction with Rickmansworth Road. The lodge to Chorleywood House is in the distance. The main road was improved for the Marquis of Salisbury to enable him to travel from Hatfield House to take the 'cure' at Bath and the route became known locally as 'the Gout Road'.

Chorleywood House – a view of the old mansion built on the site of an ancient farm in 1822 by John Barnes, a wealthy stockbroker. Members of the Saunders Gilliat family resided here in the days of Queen Victoria. The estate was purchased in 1892 by Lady Russell, who demolished the house seen here and built a more modern residence on the site. The estate was bought by the Chorleywood Urban District Council in the late 1940s.

It is not often that a view remains unchanged from the early days of this century. But Loudwater Hill, off the main Chorleywood Road, still looks like this. It was constructed in the 1880s and was then called Longfoot Hill.

Loudwater House was built in 1825 by Joseph Samada, the MP for Tower Hamlets, as a country retreat. A well known engineer, he was associated with the early days of the Metropolitan Railway.

Loudwater House eventually became the home of Panmure Gordon, another wealthy City man. He liked the good life and gave lavish parties here, even running a horse-drawn coach to take guests to the races at Windsor.

Loudwater House and the ornamental bridge as it appeared in 1914.

In 1924 the estate was purchased by Cameron Jeffs, the house was converted into flats and the estate lands were partly developed for high class housing. A brochure published in the early 1930s rather over-reached itself in selling the virtues of living amid the wooded delights of the Chess Valley: 'It's the trees, the fairy dingles and a hundred and one things which dame nature's fingers have lingered long in setting out this beautiful display of trout stream, wooded slopes, meadow and hill top sites… send a postcard today for the homestead of your dreams'.

The lake at Loudwater, created from the waters of the River Chess by Penmure Gordon. He also laid out the grounds with many rare trees.

The lake and the River Chess. In the 1930s fine villas began to be built, carefully hidden amongst the trees, which comprised the Loudwater Troutstream Estate and the Loudwater (Bridle Lane) Estates Limited. Adjacent to Loudwater was the Glen Chess estate. The house was built around 1849 by Herbert Ingram, founder of the Illustrated London News and he laid out the banks of the River Chess here with shrubs and fine trees. In 1913, a guide book stated that '…the grounds were open on Wednesdays and Thursdays, thanks to the public spirit of Mr Wilson Young.'

On the south side of Rickmansworth Road and the Common is The Cedars estate. When this photograph was taken by the Watford photographer, Coles in 1905, it was the home of James Saunders Gilliat, an MP and JP. He had bought the estate in 1860 and rebuilt the eighteenth century house. He did not like the nearby public house, the Finch's Arms, because he felt it 'lowered the social tone.' So he had it rebuilt as the Black Horse out on the Common by Appletree Dell.

Two views of King John's Farm in Shire Lane, which dates back to the fifteenth century. It was here, on 4 April 1672, that William Penn married Guliema Springett, daughter of Sir William Springett of Brayles Park, Ringmere, Sussex.

CHORLEY WOOD, KING JOHN'S FARM HOUSE, NEAR RICKMANSWORTH.

The farm was later owned by Arthur Capel, one of the sons of the Earl of Essex, who lived at Cassiobury Park, Watford.

Appletree Dell, with The Cedars visible to the top right. At nearby Appletree Farm was the home of great conductor Sir Henry Wood, founder of the promenade concerts. The Cedars became a school run by the Royal National Institute for the Blind. The mansion has now been converted into private flats.

The Common, with early Metroland houses on the high ground by Shire Lane. Some of the earliest residences on the Common itself are said to have originated as the simple homes of the navvies and their families when the Metropolitan Railway was built in the 1880s.

107

Chorleywood goods yard closed in 1967 and many more houses have been built on the hill since then. One of the very first of what we call 'commuters' today was the architect and designer C.F. Voysey (1857-1941). He built himself The Orchard, which has been called the prototype of the twentieth century suburban house.

'The Common stands in a most advantageous position and, with its high elevation, renders its atmosphere as fresh and as bracing as the sea breezes' (guide book 1912). The goods yard can be seen in the foreground and, just above the signal box, the first of the new shops.

Early suburban Chorleywood. The new villas of Edwardian days rise along Shire Lane. It was Sir John Betjeman who said of the 'new' Chorleywood, 'Woodsmoke mingled with sulphur fumes... and people now could catch an early train to London and be home just after tea.'

The approach to the station with W. Darvell's coal office. The hotel is now named The Sportsman.

Ideal Metroland! Golf, horse riding, country walks and bracing air – and the home of one's dreams. It is 1913, and a commuter makes his way to the station. The houses on the left rise up to Colleyland and the Common. The name comes from Colliers Field.

The Cedars estate was developed by the Metropolitan Railway Country Estates from the 1920s and the company stressed that, 'the estate will be laid out with village greens and open spaces: well made roads... part of the beautiful woods will be kept in their natural state'.

The Cedars was the largest of the Metropolitan estates, running from the edge of Rickmansworth to beyond Chorleywood station. The first part of The Cedars' land was bought in 1922 for £40,000 and further acres were added over the next few years. The architect of this typical house was C.W. Clark, who also designed some of the Railway's more modern stations.

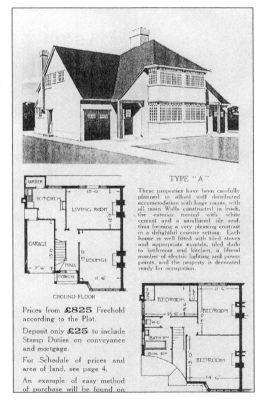

TYPE "A"

These properties have been carefully planned to afford well distributed accommodation with large rooms, with all main Walls constructed in brick, the exterior treated with white cement and a sandfaced tile roof, thus forming a very pleasing contrast in a delightful country setting. Each house is well fitted with tiled stoves and appropriate mantels, tiled dado to bathroom and kitchen, a liberal number of electric lighting and power points, and the property is decorated ready for occupation.

Prices from **£825** Freehold according to the Plot.

Deposit only **£25** to include Stamp Duties on conveyance and mortgage.

For Schedule of prices and area of land, see page 4.

An example of easy method of purchase will be found on

LOCAL DATA, &c.

relating to

NEASDEN, WEMBLEY PARK, PINNER, RICKMANSWORTH & CHORLEY WOOD Districts.

	Distance to Baker Street	Trains each way daily	Journey time to Baker Street	Altitude above sea level	Subsoil
	miles		minutes	feet	
Neasden	6	188	11	127	Gravel & Clay
Wembley Park ...	6½	101	11½	234	Clay
Pinner	11¼	35	23	163 230	Clay
Rickmansworth ...	17½	40	30	150 270	Gravel & Chalk
Chorley Wood ...	19½	36	38	368	Gravel & Chalk

	Local Rates	Gas per therm	Water	Electric Light
Neasden	16/1	10d.	8 % on Rates	6d. less 5 %
Chalk Hill ...	15/6	10d.	7 % plus extras plus 60 %	7d.
Pinner	9/6	1/2	7 % ditto	10d.
Rickmansworth ...	13/6	1/6	7½ %	10d.
Chorley Wood ...	10/10	1/8	7½ %	10d.

Information sheet issued by the Metropolitan Railway Estates in 1927. Would be purchasers were also assured that the higher priced houses would be kept separate from the lower valued property. Living at Chorleywood in the late 1930s. It was, perhaps, a little ironic that the developers wrote that, '…this modern residential settlement with many nice middle-class houses offers the freedom from anything suggestive of suburbia. A place estimed for those who desire fresh, pure air, a bracing climate and rural peace'.

Few new residents in those days would have had their own car and public transport was not very frequent, many local traders would deliver to the door. Here is Palmers of Rickmansworth somewhere on the Cedars Estate in 1934.

Mill End and the Uxbridge Road, a postcard view published by E.P. Andrews, stationer and draper of Mill End, 1914. Uxbridge Road was formerly Mill End Road, the present name being adopted in 1898.

Mill End and the Rose and Crown. All the houses on the left hand side have long been demolished for road widening, but the public house remains, appropriately called The Tree. The most important industry for many years here was watercress cultivation. The cress would be sent daily to the London markets, taken to Rickmansworth station and on the Great Central (late LNER) trains to Marylebone.

Drayton Ford, Springwell Lane, on the River Colne, just before the river was culverted in 1912. The lane leads to Springwell Lock on the canal, and the flooded gravel pit – Springwell Lake. There is also a waterworks here. In the inter-war years the Springwell Water Company manufactured soya bean flour.

No traffic to be seen in Maple Cross in the early 1920s. The present public house called the Cross was known as The Maple Cross until about 1843. Maple is probably a corruption of 'Mapull Crosse', mentioned in a local document of 1500.

Six

Croxley, Moor Park and Batchworth

Scot's Hill, looking down towards the bridge. Both Scot's Bridge and Scot's Hill were named after a Simon Skote, landowner in the time of Edward II. Scotsbridge Mill was producing paper in 1757, but closed in 1905. The building seen on the left is part of Scot's bridge.

Croxley Green and All Saints church, of which the first Lord Ebury laid the foundation stone on 27 September 1870. The land was bought from Gonville and Caius College, Cambridge and the building was consecrated on 25 June 1827. Enlarged in 1907 to meet the needs of a growing area, it had the misfortune to be badly damaged by bombs in September 1940.

Croxley Green Metropolitan Railway station soon after it was opened in 1925. It was designed to 'harmonise with the local surroundings' (according to a press announcement of that year). A yard was provided for handling coal and general freight. The station name was changed to Croxley on 23 May 1949.

The top of Scot's Hill and Ward's the grocers, where tea is for sale at 1/6d. The shop was also the post office. The row of cottages was known as Penny Row (the original rent paid weekly by the elderly residents). After the First World War, the cottages were let to ex-servicemen for 3/- a week and local people changed the unofficial name to Heroes' Row. They were demolished in around 1926.

117

Croxley Green and the Artichoke public house, with the sign of The Coach and Horses in the distance.

Looking south near the Artichoke, with Horfield Cottage and 'Southview' on the left. The tree was later replaced by the Jubilee Oak, planted in 1935, which commemorated twenty five years of the reign of King George V.

The northern end of Croxley Green, near Croxley House. Much of the Green (once called Common Moor) would have disappeared had a proposed railway from Watford to Uxbridge (via Rickmansworth) been built in the 1860s. A meeting was held at the Artichoke on 20 February 1861 to discuss terms for the proposed extinguishing of Commoners' rights.

The pond near Waterwell House at the northern end of the Green in around 1910.

John Dickinson and his paper making empire were very much part of Croxley and they built Dickinson Square and Avenue in the 1890s for their employees. This photograph shows the Dickinson Institute, a social and cultural centre which had started in a nearby cottage.

A group of wounded servicemen outside the Dickinson Institute during the First World War. The building was demolished in 1976.

Both New Road and Watford Road were lined with all kinds of houses, cottages and small shops long before the Metropolitan Railway station was opened in 1925. Dimmock's store is typical of many local shops. The offices on the left hand side of this tiny building is that of the parcel agent for the London and North Western Railway at Watford.

The old road to London at the foot of Batchworth hill. The inn is the Queen's Head. In the First World War, German prisoners were used to help widen the road.

Moor Park, Rickmansworth.

If Rickmansworth Park dominated the town centre, Moor Park dominated the eastern side of the town. 'Moor Park, the sweetest place, I think, that I have seen in my life, at home or abroad' wrote Sir William Temple in 1785. The house we see today was built in 1678-79 for James, Duke of Monmouth. It was reconstructed in the style we see here by James Thornhill for Benjamin Styles in 1720.

It was the 1920s that made Moor Park a place to build a 'sheltered seat'. Lord Ebury sold the estate to Lord Luvershulme's property development company. 'Here one may enjoy quietude and seclusion (without isolation) with all the amenities of residence in an old English Park'. Here was a chance to live the life of a country gentleman without the worries of servants and large grounds. An ideal Metroland – with tea on the terrace and endless tennis and golf.

MOOR PARK ESTATE

TWENTY-FIVE MINUTES FROM TOWN

Frequent through expresses to and from the City.

The Estate is an unspoiled historic old English park, being developed in a manner to preserve and protect its delightful scenery, and thus combine the facilities of London with the rural amenities of the County of Hertford.

MAIN DRAINAGE	SAND and GRAVEL SUBSOIL

Price **FREEHOLD £2,225**

Golf and residences of distinction at Moor Park 1930. The golf course was laid out in the 1920s to the plans of H.S. Colt. 'There will be few inland courses better than that... at Moor Park'.

Price FREEHOLD £2,275

| ELECTRIC | GAS |
| LIGHT | CONNECTED |

The above are typical examples of the houses erected and in course of erection at Moor Park, designed in the inexpensive efficient style of modern architecture, blending utility of accommodation with attractiveness of elevation.

ILLUSTRATIONS AND PLANS OF THESE AND OTHER HOUSES AT MOOR PARK

contained in a booklet which also describes the three eighteen hole golf courses, magnificent Club House, tennis courts, etc.

MAY BE HAD ON APPLICATION

by letter, phone or a personal visit to the Estate, from the

Estate Manager, Moor Park, HERTS

Phone : Rickmansworth 217.

SAY YOU SAW IT IN "METRO-LAND."

Illustration from Metroland 1927 advertising the advantages of coming to live at Moor Park. These benefits included fast electric expresses to the heart of the City and the pleasures of playing on the Moor Park courses or the adjacent Sandy Lodge course (north of the railway).

'Accessibility has a real meaning when applied to Moor Park in relation to easy travel to London'. Prospective residents at Moor Park were offered all the delights of a land of lobelias and tennis flannels in 1931.

Opposite: Batchworth Heath House as it appeared in 1923. The house was the home of Sir Robert and Lady Morier. He was a famous British ambassador in the nineteenth century. He was buried at Northwood in November 1893 and the Czar of Russia gave a memorial urn for his tomb.

MOOR PARK
Residential Estate

Beautifully Wooded Heights
PROTECTED
DEVELOPMENT
Three 18 Hole Golf Courses.
Hard & Grass Tennis Courts.
Delightful Country Club.

Particulars of Choice Freehold Building Sites from The Estate Office, The Club House, Moor Park and the Principal Agents.

Looking up Batchworth Hill towards Batchworth Heath. A three-wheeled light car can be seen near Home Farm as can the edge of the grounds of Moor Park in this view from around 80 years ago.

The Green Man was first recorded in 1728 when Richard Ryder was landlord. A century ago, the blacksmith's forge stood next door. It was at one time run by Alfred Hudgkinson, known as 'The Strong Man of Hertfordshire'. He was an extraordinary character and there is a story of how he once refused to pay for his donkey at the Northwood Toll Gate, carrying the amazed animal across instead!

Moor Park Arch and the old cottages at the top of Batchworth Lane in the days when Lord Ebury lived at the great house.

A general view of Batchworth Heath in 1902. The gateway on the left is to Moor Park. The road to the right is White Hill, leading to Harefield. The hamlet of Batchworth Heath was probably the original settlement of Northwood, which lies just over the border in Middlesex.

For our last picture, we cross the border into Middlesex on the edge of Batchworth Heath to Mount Vernon. The hospital came here from Hampstead and the foundation stone was laid on 13 May 1902. The hospital had been originally founded for the 'relief of the consumptive poor'. It later became a general hospital. This view dates from around 1929. In the distance is the Colne valley and Mill End, a landscape that was then unspoiled by gravel lakes, industry and busy roadways. Fortunately, much of the land seen here remains part of the London green belt.

The old steep hill down into Rickmansworth from Batchworth has long ceased to be the main road. Improvements were carried out to the old roadway here by German prisoners during the First World War. This picture was taken in 1922.

Printed in Great Britain
by Amazon